Heroic Personal Finances

3 Steps To Become A Money Hero

LARRY JONES

First Edition: May 2017

ISBN-10: 154655162X
ISBN-13: 978-1546551621

For additional information on the book *Heroic Personal Finances: 3 Steps to Become a Money Hero* and to receive a FREE Healthy Personal Finances Checklist, visit HeroicPersonalFinances.com.

Cover Design by: pixelrocket on Fiverr®

CONTENTS

DISCLAIMER

The intention of this book is for informational and motivational purposes only. It was sold with the understanding that the author is not bound to give any financial, legal, psychological, or any other type of professional advice. The information and actions proposed in this book are not intended as a substitute for counseling. The author will not be liable for any physical, psychological, emotional, financial, or commercial damages. The reader must test everything for his or herself according to their unique situation, talents, finances, and aspirations. Each person is responsible for his or her decisions, choices, actions, and results.

This book is a synthesis of ideas taken from several different personal finance and self-help sources. Any third party sources mentioned in this book may include products and opinions expressed by their owners. As such, the author does not assume responsibility or liability for any third party sources. The fact that certain individuals, organizations, or websites are mentioned does not mean the author endorses the information or recommendations these individuals, organizations, or websites may make. Also, readers should be aware that any website listed in this book may have changed or disappeared between the time the book was written and when it is read.

The author did his due diligence and made every effort to ensure the information presented in this book was correct at press time. Therefore, the author does not assume any liability to any party for any loss, damage, or disruption caused by errors or omissions, whether such errors or omissions result from negligence, accident, or any other cause. No warranty may be created or extended by sales representatives or written sales materials. The advice and strategies contained in this book may not be suitable for every person's unique situation; consult with a professional when appropriate.

The rights to any trademarks, quotes, and excerpts from books, movies, TV shows, brands, or other media mentioned in this publication belong to their respective owners. As such, they are presented in this book according to fair use doctrine.

No part of this publication may be reproduced, transmitted, or sold in whole or in part in any form, without the prior written consent of the

HEALTHY PERSONAL FINANCES CHECKLIST FREE DOWNLOAD

Interested in learning more about becoming a hero with your money? Download a FREE, 23-page Healthy Personal Finances Checklist, at heroicpersonalfinances.com.

INTRODUCTION

If you wrote down some of the biggest personal finance problems that people face today, what would you say those problems are? Maybe your list would include such challenges as a lack of income, crushing debt load, expensive health care, no family budget, or lack of knowledge?

Yes, these are all big problems in today's world of personal finances. But, I believe we can simplify this answer. We can distil it down to one problem: **we don't have enough money heroes in our lives.**

Everybody needs a hero. Everybody needs a guide to show them the way.

In the *Star Wars* movies, Luke Skywalker had Master Yoda. In the original *Karate Kid* movies, Daniel-san had Mr. Miyagi. Robin had Batman. Even Superman had crystal recordings of his dad Jor-El in the Fortress of Solitude.

We all need a hero. We all need a guide to show us the way.

Let's take a moment and define the word "hero." A hero is a person noted for courageous acts or nobility of character; a person who, in the opinion of others, has special achievements, abilities, or personal qualities. A hero is regarded as a role model or ideal.[i]

There are two parts to this definition that I would like to stress. First, the hero has achieved something. He has taken action and accomplished a courageous act. Second, a hero is considered a role model. They are the ideal to look up to in a particular area of life.

For the last fourteen years, several money heroes have made an impression in my life. People such as Ron Blue, Dave Ramsey, Robert Kiyosaki, Robert G. Allen, David Bach, Tony Robbins, and many others. I've consumed their books. I've attended their seminars. I've listened to their podcasts. I've watched their videos.

I've learned a lot about money from these money masters through immersing myself into their financial knowledge. I have "cherry picked" the best of their advice and applied it to my family's finances. I am wealthier today as a result of implementing their wisdom.

Through reading this book, allow me to be your guide as I share with you what I have learned over the last several years. I believe you have the potential to become the hero of your money story. Together, let's make this a reality for you and your family.

To your financial success!

STEP #1
CAPTURE THE VISION,
THEN MAKE A DECISION

"Where there is no vision, the people perish." – Proverbs 29:18, KJV[ii]

"Everything begins with a decision. Then, we have to manage that decision for the rest of your life." – John Maxwell[iii]

In 2004, I was walking through a Barnes and Noble bookstore and passed the money and business section. A blueish-green book caught my eye. I walked over and picked it up. The title of the book was *Financial Peace* written by some author named Dave Ramsey. I had never heard of him before that time.

The book looked interesting enough, so I bought the book and took it home. I ended up reading the book in a day or two. It was a super fast, easy read.

As a result of reading that book, my mind was blown away with a vision of possibility. I received a new money vision of becoming debt free, paying our bills on time, having money in the bank, and having financial peace in the life of my family.

There's an old proverb in the Bible that says, "Without a vision, the people perish" (Proverbs 29:18). This saying is just as true today as it was when King Solomon penned it thousands of years ago. Life purpose and meaning flow out of a vision for anything. This vision isn't just about money. A vision for every area of life, whether it be marriage, family, health, career, or business can be a powerful tool to propel one forward in the direction they want to go.

With no vision, though, we tend to remain stuck. We tread water. We have no direction. We have little drive to do anything or be anything. A vision is necessary to achieve anything in life. Over the next few chapters, let's go deeper on capturing an incredible vision for our personal finances. Then, let's make a decision that we are no longer satisfied with staying stuck in the status quo when it comes to money. Make a decision right now to dream bigger in the area of personal finances.

CHAPTER 1
THE VISION THING

The year was 1987. George Herbert Walker Bush was Vice President in the Reagan White House. President Reagan's second term was coming to an end, and both political parties were gearing up for the next election cycle in 1988.

Vice President Bush was giving every sign to the Republican party that he planned on running for the presidential nomination. He had one major challenge, though. Bush had difficulty articulating the direction he wanted to take the country if the people elected him as President. He struggled with a vision for the nation.

One of his friends encouraged him to go to Camp David for several days to get alone and get clear on a direction for the country. Bush said to his friend in apparent exasperation, "Oh, you mean the vision thing." The Vice President was not impressed with his friend's advice.

In many ways, George H. W. Bush is fortunate that one statement alone didn't sink his election bid. His enemies did use it against him and painted him as a "wimp." Fortunately for Bush, he was able to ride the long coattails of a popular President Reagan straight into the White House. At a different time in history, though, a statement such as that would have been a death knell for his election.

The wimp factor and "vision thing" did come back to haunt President Bush in the 1992 election cycle. Bush still could not articulate a vision why people should re-elect him. His Democrat rival Bill Clinton, though, could paint a vision of possibility around his presidency - hope and change. As a result of this clear vision, Clinton defeated Bush. Even the Bush bio posted on the official U.S. Senate website says:

"Bush...suffered from his lack of what he called 'the vision thing,' a clarity of ideas and principles that could shape public opinion and influence Congress. 'He does not say why he wants to be there,' complained columnist George Will, 'so the public does not know why it should care if he gets his way.'"[iv]

By contrast, actor Sylvester Stallone had an incredible vision for his life.

He stuck to his principles even in the most difficult of circumstances. Because of his vision, he ended up receiving what he desired.

As a boy, Stallone grew up with the deck stacked against him. He had slurred speech and facial deformities as a result of a facial nerve that was severed during birth. He bounced around various foster families. The foster system sent him to a high school for troubled kids.

During his twenties, he tried his hand at acting, but he could not break through. Stallone ended up working in a deli. He was so poor that he ended up living in a bus shelter for a time.

His big break came after watching a boxing match where the unknown underdog Chuck Wepner took world champion Muhammed Ali to 15 rounds in the ring. Stallone went home and within three days wrote the first draft to the movie *Rocky*. He then went out and pitched the movie to several different studios. There was immediate interest. These studios wanted to buy the script from Stallone. He wouldn't sell, though, unless these studios gave him the lead role in his movie.

He stuck to his guns, too. Even after one studio offered $325,000 for his script, he refused. Stallone knew this was his big break. He had a vision. For him, this was all or nothing. One of the studios finally consented. They bought his script for $35,000 and allowed him to play the lead for award wages. The rest is history. *Rocky* was a blockbuster movie, and Stallone became a star as a result.

A vision is important. Whether one is running for President or creating an ideal life, vision will be the difference maker.

CHAPTER 2
BURN THE SHIPS!

Vision is necessary, but vision will only take a person so far. At some point, one has to make a decision to move forward with that vision. Leadership guru John Maxwell said this, "Everything begins with a decision. Then, we have to manage that decision for the rest of your life."[v]

Everything begins with a decision. Ponder that statement for a moment. Anything achieved in life all started with a decision. People who have been obese and lost a bunch of weight all began with a vision of being thin and then making a decision to be thin. Couples who have struggled in their marriages and made a relationship turnaround captured a vision of a happy marriage. They made a decision to act on their vision. People who have caught the vision of a successful business and made it a reality had to make a decision to do so. These things usually don't happen by accident.

When you were a student in school, you most likely read the story of Spanish explorer Captain Hernando Cortez. In 1519, Cortez landed 500 soldiers, 100 sailors, and 11 ships on the shores of the Yucatan to begin his great conquest of the Aztec people. His primary goal was to seize the treasure of the Aztecs. This goal was ambitious for Cortez because the Aztecs outnumbered this small Spanish fighting force by the thousands.

Unconvinced they could win, a small group of Cortez's men attempted to seize some of the ships to sail back to the safety of Cuba. Cortez found out about the mutinous plot and rounded up the ringleaders. To keep unity with the remaining men, Cortez ordered the unthinkable - scuttle all the ships by burning them. He saved only one ship to take back part of the Aztec treasure to the king of Spain.

In Cortez's mind, this was an all or nothing scenario. By burning the ships, he left no escape plan. They had to defeat the Aztecs and take the treasure or die trying. No retreats. No turning back. As a result of this brilliant move, Cortez inspired his men to go to the next level of commitment to win, and they did![vi]

At the beginning of this first section of the book, I shared part of my personal finance story. As a result of reading the original *Financial Peace* book, I captured a vision of what could be possible in the area of my family's personal finances. Instinctively, though, I knew that vision wasn't going to be enough. I knew I had to make a decision that living in our old financial patterns of debt and overspending wasn't going to create that new vision.

I made zero excuses. I made no way to fall back to our old way of doing personal finances. This vision was an "all or nothing" proposition with our money. We either figure out this personal finance thing or else. We pay off all our debts and get into a better financial position for the sake of our family or else.

We captured a beautiful vision of possibility with our personal finances. Then, we made a decision to figure out how to make this new vision a reality. We are not turning back to our old money habits. We are moving forward to financial victory and wealth

CHAPTER 3
WHAT IS YOUR FINANCIAL VISION?

Do you have a vision for what you want to achieve in your personal finances? Do you want to be debt free? Do you want to have all your bills paid each month without going through a money fight with your spouse? Would you like to have money sitting in the bank for a rainy day reserve fund? Would you like to have multiple streams of income flowing into your life that make you wealthier, even while you sleep? Would you like to own investment real estate? Would you like to own your own business? Would you like to be a generous giver to your favorite charities in ever increasing amounts?

I know in my life, my vision began quite simple at first: get debt free, have all the bills paid on time every month, and get some money saved in the bank. And then, over the course of two years of that vision becoming a reality, my vision began to expand even larger. As I grew in my knowledge of personal finances and wealth building, the image morphed over time.

Vision is powerful, but a vision is never enough in and of itself. Once you have a strong vision, you have to make that final decision that you don't want to live the same way anymore. You can't go back to the old way of doing things. You have to move toward your vision because of a new belief system.

Get a compelling vision for your financial future, then make a decision to go toward that new vision as fast as possible. Once you arrive, be open to an even loftier vision to take you to a higher level in your personal finances.

CHALLENGE

Do you have an all-encompassing financial vision for your life? Do you know where you are heading in your finances and why? Have you ever made a decision that you are fed up with where you currently are in life? Are you willing to make the changes necessary to fulfill your vision?

Download your free worksheets that go with the chapters of this book. Go to www.heroicpersonalfinances.com/3stepsworkbook.

STEP #2
CREATE A PLAN, THEN TAKE ACTION

"Take time to deliberate; but when the time for action arrives, stop thinking and go in." - Andrew Jackson[vii]

"Losers have goals. Winners have systems." – Scott Adams[viii]

In the first step to become a hero with money, we saw why we need to capture a vision for our finances. Then, we need to make a decision that we will no longer live out the same old useless patterns with our money.

The second step takes us to the next level. This level is the practical, hands-on approach, where doing something moves us into our vision and decision. We are now acting upon the changes that have taken place in our minds.

Tony Robbins, the famous self-help guru, says "Setting goals is the first step in turning the invisible into the visible."[ix] Goals are the roadmap to success.

When my family and I were transmuting our new financial vision into reality, we had to have an action plan. At the time, this meant we were working through the baby steps as prescribed in Financial Peace University™. First, we built up $1,000 in our savings account as fast as possible. The purpose of this money is for a small emergency fund to kick our dependence on credit cards. Second, we listed our debts from smallest to largest. Then, with any extra money in the budget, we attacked each debt until we paid them off. We moved down our debts list as fast as possible. Dave Ramsey calls this the debt snowball.

After we had paid off all our consumer debts (credit cards, car loans, and student loans), we moved into the third baby step. We put three to six months worth of budget expense money into savings for a large emergency fund. For example, if a family needs $5,000 a month to keep all their bills paid (mortgage, utilities, insurances, gas, food, etc.), then this family's target amount in a bank account will be $15,000-$30,000.

We had a clear step-by-step system laid before us to follow. Having the plan was necessary, but executing the plan was key. Nothing happens without execution. In Step #2, we will discuss creating and taking action on these financial plans.

CHAPTER 4
DO AN 80/20 ANALYSIS ON MONEY

Have you ever heard of the Pareto principle? It's also known as the 80/20 Rule. This concept was named after economist Vilfredo Pareto. He discovered the unequal relationship between inputs and outputs. This discovery was a result of Pareto doing research on the distribution of wealth within a country. What he found in the country he studied is that 20% of the people controlled 80% of the money.

You can discover this imbalance of inputs and outputs in almost anything in life. For example, in your work or business life, accomplishing the right 20% of your job activities could produce 80% of your work related output. In your personal time management, the correct 20% of your daily actions will end up giving you 80% of your desired results. In your relationships, the right 20% of your communication and activities will give you 80% of your needs and desires.

The same goes with money. If one can figure out the top 20% of personal finance habits that can lead to 80% of desired results, then a wealthy life will be the result over time. In putting together a financial plan, one needs to be sensitive to what exactly could give them that 80/20 leverage. My suggestion would be to do some investigative research on the 20% of activities that leads to 80% of results for the wealthy.

If I wrote down my top 20% of activities that lead to winning financially, it would uncover several key factors. First, filling out a consistent budget form at the beginning of each month would be at the top of that list. Second, utilizing cash instead of debit or credit cards for everyday purchases such as dining out and groceries. Using cash forces you to stay on target with your budget plan. Third, getting out of any and all consumer debt as fast as possible and staying debt free. Fourth, focusing on maximizing time, energy, and output on all our income streams. Fifth, minimizing taxes paid each year with all legitimate deductions. I religiously keep records and receipts on file to help me at tax time each year. Sixth, automating my family's personal finances as much as possible. Financial automation includes such items as direct deposit for multiple income streams, auto payment of utilities and credit cards, and weekly automated charitable giving to our church and other charities. A few years ago, I spent several hours setting up these automated systems on the front end. Now, I save time and hassle dealing with monthly bills. All I need to do now is watch transactions going in and out of our bank accounts. I will talk more about this in Step #3.

If you think about it, the 80/20 Pareto Principle steps that I list above are a series of money practices I have incorporated into my life. Quality habits are the key to accomplishing anything amazing in your life.

CHAPTER 5
WEALTHY HABITS

If you read somewhere that becoming wealthy is the result of daily habits, routines, and systems, what would you say? Maybe you would say, "No way that's true? That can't be possible? I don't believe it?"

Well, believe it or not, the research seems to support this fact. The majority of the wealthy become wealthy through establishing a set of particular habits in their daily lives. Most rich people don't become wealthy because of a money fairy, luck, the lottery, or a large inheritance. The vast majority of wealthy people arrive at wealth through a series of rich habits.

Most people don't like hearing this answer, and here's why. If you can become wealthy by incorporating a set of habits into your daily life, then this means that all of us are not only responsible but capable of being wealthier today than we are right now. Every one of us has to accept full responsibility for our current level of wealth.

For example, the research seems to bear out the fact that a day in the life of the wealthy looks something like this. First, they get up early. The average rich person wakes up three hours before they leave for their regular 9-to-5 job. So what do they do in those three hours before work? They focus on self-improvement activities such as reading, writing, thinking, meditating, working out, and more. They recognize that while the rest of the world sleeps, they use this quiet, focused time to become a better, more productive person through a series of positive habits and routines. Doing this day in and day out over several years has an exponential effect on the results these people can achieve.

Second, once the wealthy begin their regular 9-to-5 work, they enter that daily work time with extreme focus. These people are clear on the top two or three priorities they need to complete to be successful in their job. They keep a "to do" list and can usually check off 70% of the items on their list. The wealthy tend to avoid long, leisurely lunches. If they do go to lunch, they are using it as an opportunity to network with other people.

Third, when they eat throughout the day, they tend to watch what they put in their body. The wealthy attempt to avoid junk food and too much alcohol consumption. They try to live out a healthy lifestyle.

Fourth, relationships are important to the wealthy. When they leave work in the evening, they make every attempt to leave their job at the workplace. They want to focus on their families at home. They enjoy spending time and doing activities with their spouse and children.

Fifth, they tend to avoid time wasters such as TV watching and internet consumption at home. They typically watch less than an hour of TV per day and avoid jumping on social media apps throughout the day. The wealthy engage in self-improvement activities such as reading books. As the old saying goes, "readers are leaders."

There is a path to wealth. The research states that most wealthy people become wealthy through a series of consistent, daily, positive habits and routines. Want to be more prosperous in life? Work on your habits, first.

CHAPTER 6
AREAS TO PLAN

When it comes to personal finances, there are several parts to think about in your planning. In this section, I'll touch on a few of the main areas to consider.

First, everyone needs a budget, and we all need to create a new cash flow plan each month (you can always use the same budget template, though!). Why? The reason is each month has different expenses in varying amounts. One may also have variable income from month to month. One needs to account for this type of revenue as well. I will cover more on budgeting in the next section, Step #3. Setting up checking account auto-drafts for bills is also a wise move for cash flow plans. There's the old saying that "time is money." For me, I don't like wasting a bunch of time each month sitting at my desk paying bills when I could be doing something a lot more productive.

Second, we need to have a savings plan. I'll use my savings system as an example. There is nothing sacred about my plan. This savings plan is how I chose to set up my family's strategy. We have a small emergency reserve fund in our local bank of approximately $2,000. The purpose of this small reserve fund is to catch any monthly emergencies such as car and minor home repairs. We also have a larger reserve fund of approximately three months worth of expense money in an online savings account. This larger reserve fund pays a higher interest rate. The goal is never to touch this money if possible. We also have an actual cash reserve fund in a safe at home. The purpose of this cash reserve fund is for extreme emergencies when banking is not available. We connect this reserve fund to our survival plan. Also related to both a savings and survival strategy is the concept of "freezing your fruit" through purchasing gold and silver. This approach is a good way to protect a part of your assets that retains its value through periods of high inflation.

Third, we should have a giving strategy. For my family, we give to our local church a little more than 10% of our income. We also give smaller amounts monthly to a couple of other charitable organizations. Again, just like our bills being auto drafted, we do the same with our giving. We account for all our charitable giving in our budget plan. We automate our giving through our checking account.

Fourth, we need to have a survival strategy. Do I think we will ever have some major earth catastrophe that will cause us to hold up in our homes for months on end? I would say anything is possible but unlikely. There's a greater chance a major weather event could cause us problems for several days. Inclement weather has displaced my family in the past when a major ice storm hit my hometown and knocked out power to my house for two weeks! At the time, my family had no emergency backup plan at all. Today is a different story. We own a large generator. We have extra fuel. We own emergency food supplies. We have extra water in storage. We have emergency cash on hand. We hope we never need these emergency supplies. We can relax in a place of knowing that if something were to happen, we have covered our basic needs.

Fifth, we should have an insurance strategy. We need to make sure that we have the proper amount of life insurance to take care of our families if we were to die at a young age. We need affordable car insurance that has the best liability and comprehensive coverage possible. We need affordable, quality health insurance in a time where this is becoming more important. If we are renters, we need renter's insurance to cover the loss of our belongings. If we are homeowners, we need quality homeowner's insurance to cover damage to structure and belongings. Finally, as we get older (around age 55-60), we should consider long-term care insurance.

Sixth, we should have an investing strategy. Everyone seems to have investment advice. Some of it is legitimate. A lot of it is not worth listening to. I'll be honest. I don't have all the answers when it comes to investing advice. I'm always reading online articles and books, attempting to fine tune my family's investment strategy. I'll share a few thoughts with you here. One, wealthy people own tangible assets of value. These assets include precious metals, real estate, and cash value life insurance products. Some of these assets may only keep pace with inflation, but they're also not paper fiat money either. They hold real financial value over time. Two, don't always believe the investing advice of your average financial guru in books, radio, and TV. They tend to focus on buying certain percentages of various mutual funds in your 401(k) and IRAs. Mutual funds are not always the best products to build long-term wealth. Third, start out as a conservative investor and take on more risk as you learn and grow. One of the best tools that I've run across to help me grow as an investor is the investment pyramid. If you do a Google search on investment pyramid, you will receive many different examples. Each example is someone else's interpretation of this fundamental concept. Here's a quick summary of the pyramid: conservative investing takes place at the bottom of the pyramid; risky investing is at the top. When beginning to invest, start at the base of the pyramid and work your way over time to the top of the pyramid. The challenge many amateur investors have is bypassing the traditional forms of investing. They hedge all their bets at the top of the pyramid. Check out a blog post I wrote on this topic here: go to heroicpersonalfinances.com. In the search function, type in "investment pyramid," and you will go straight to that post.

Seventh, we need to have a business strategy. The wealthy are entrepreneurs. There are a lot of great reasons to start, own, or buy a business. There are tax benefits to running a business. There are cash flow generation benefits to running a business. Find a hobby or side passion you believe you could turn into a legitimate business over time. Keep working your full-time job and invest as much time, energy, and money into your side hustle as possible. See if you can make your side hustle your new full-time position.

Eighth, we need to make sure we have taken care of our estate planning. I used to think that having a will was enough to avoid probate court. A few years ago, our attorney put together end of life legal documents for my wife and me: Last Will and Testament, Durable Power of Attorney, and Living Will Health Care Directive. While better than nothing, these documents will still allow the courts to probate your estate plan when you die. I recently learned that a better estate planning strategy to use is a living trust. Understand up front that a living trust is much more expensive than a will. The benefit for your family, though, is that the majority of living trusts will avoid the need for court. Pay a little bit more now on the front end, or your family could end up paying a lot more when they have to straighten out your estate mess in court.

Ninth, we need to create legal strategies to protect and grow our wealth. I've already touched on a few of them already. Establishing a living trust for your end of life planning is a great start. Also, creating an LLC business is another tool in the toolbox. I am not an expert in this particular area. I recommend reading the book *Multiple Streams of Income: How To Generate A Lifetime Of Unlimited Wealth*, Second Edition by Robert G. Allen. In Chapter 17, he shares some interesting Financial Fortress Strategies you can use to shield your financial life.

CHAPTER 7
TALK IS CHEAP

We live in a time when people like to talk a lot about solutions to problems, but few people seem willing to roll up their sleeves and take action. I understand. I used to be the same way since I was a teenager. I would talk a good game. I would make plans, and then I would create intentions to accomplish a big goal in my life. After that, I would do nothing, except maybe make more plans.

I thought by the mere act of preparing for a specific goal that I was accomplishing something great. The reality is that planning means nothing until action and completion take place. The strange thing for me is that this important concept of action and completion didn't sink into my brain until I reached mid-life. Now that I understand the importance of execution and completion, I find myself focused on doing this for any and all projects in which I am involved.

Take writing this book as an example. Do you know what the statistics are for people who desire to write a book versus the ones who publish a book? Whether it's self-published or released by a publisher doesn't matter. What's the percentage of authors who cross the finish line from book idea to finished product?

Let's start with the numbers of people who desire to write a book. They have a vision of possibility - a published book with their name on it. After doing some quick online research, it would seem that 80-90% of Americans would like to write a book. This statistic means that eight out of every ten adults you pass by on any given day believe they have at least one book inside of them they would like to write. This number is approximately 200 million people!

What's reality, though? Out of these 200 million people, how many have the fortitude and discipline to sit down and go through the arduous process of cranking out a book and publishing it? Here are the best statistics I could uncover. Out of every 1,000 people who start writing a book, only 30 finish. Only 3% of writers complete the act of writing. I don't know about you, but that number seems pretty low to me! Even though there are millions of books and authors on book sites such as Amazon, this number only accounts for the 3% who were able to cross the finish line with their books.

There are lots of people who say they want to write a book, but talk is cheap. Shut up and put up. Do the hard work. The world doesn't owe you anything. Be part of the 3% who put action and hard work behind their words.

Do you want to achieve something great in your personal finances? Do you want to become the hero of your money story? Then you have to stop talking about it. You have to quit making more goals and plans for what you want to do. You know what you want. Time to get off your duff and take action on your vision and goals. Now is the time to become part of the small majority who make it across the finish line of accomplishment.

CHAPTER 8
SYSTEMS ARE THE KEY

Scott Adams, the creator of the famous "Dilbert" comic strip, said this, "Losers have goals. Winners have systems."[x] I believe this is what Adams meant by that statement. Written goals do nothing. As I mentioned in Chapter 7, talk is cheap. One accomplishes nothing through the act of goal setting alone. The people who win are the ones who create action systems to achieve the objective.

For example, let's say someone wrote down a goal to lose 20 pounds over the next three months. A way this person could go about putting systems in place to achieve that target might be the following. First, calculate needed weight loss per week over the three months. There are roughly twelve weeks during this time. Twenty divided by twelve equals a little less than two pounds per week (1.67 to be exact). Wow! An easy weekly goal to meet. Second, research healthy eating and exercise routines to put in place over the three months. Third, set up a healthy meal plan with a system to make it easy to install every day. Fourth, determine an exercise routine schedule and find an accountability partner to help you stay faithful. Fifth, set up schedule reminders in your phone calendar to trigger your new meal plan and exercise routine. Sixth, follow your new eating and exercise regimen. Seventh, track and record your weight loss at the end of each week. Eighth, adjust your plan based on recorded data.

If one wants to win in any area of life whether it be health, relationships, business, or personal finances, then one needs goals with systems in place to achieve these aims.

I might add here that goals and systems will morph over time. This change is both good and necessary. Although I have a general financial plan that I am following in my mind (and on paper), my primary goals and systems are short term depending on the desired outcome. For example, when my wife and I were paying off around $100,000 worth of consumer debt, I knew it would take us approximately three years to pay it off. So, during these three years, the goal was to pay off these debts with laser-like focus as fast as we could. The systems I put in place to do this were the following. First, generating multiple streams of income from a variety of extra work. Second, creating a bare-bones monthly budget, squeezing out all extra dollars to pay off debt at the end of each month. Third, setting up auto payment on all bills and debts. Fourth, writing down a debt snowball chart, listing all our debts from smallest to largest. Fifth, throwing any and all extra budget money on to the smallest debt on the snowball list each month. Sixth, working our way down that list as fast as possible. We monitored progress through our various online accounts along the way. Seventh, we celebrated becoming debt free after 35 months with dinner at a fancy, expensive restaurant!

Having written goals to win in the area of money is nice and all, but writing stuff down means nothing. You have to have a systematic action plan with focused execution to achieve those goals. For those who are into "sexy" quick fixes, they may as well just throw in the towel now. Taking action on financial goals such as this is neither fast nor sexy. Working out your financial plan takes focused determination over time.

In Chapter 5, I mentioned wealthy habits and their importance. I view that section as "micro" money habits. These are the small, daily, repetitive habits one can do over time that can make one wealthy, such as morning routines, health habits, and so on.

In this chapter, I want to focus more on the "meta" or "macro" habits that will help you take action on your financial plans. For example, let's discuss what patterns go into making a consistent monthly budget plan. The following is a system I have created that I walk through each month to help my family stay on track with our financial plan:

- A few days before a new month begins, I create a copy of my current month's estimated budget spreadsheet. I rename the copy for the next month and change key information. I put a new date at the top. I adjust any and all appropriate income and outgo numbers.

- I determine which budget categories will need cash for our envelope system. These categories include: groceries, dining out, blow money, etc.

- I calculate how many of each monetary denomination I need for each envelope system category. For example, let's say I budgeted

$500 cash for groceries for the first half of a month (first pay period). I might write down that I need three $100 bills, two $50 bills, four $20s, and two $10s. You can break this amount down any way you want. You could do twenty-five $20 bills. Whatever makes you happy!

- I break down all the money denominations for each of the cash envelopes we need to fund. I then add up how many of each denomination I need to withdraw from the bank. I write it down on a slip of paper for the bank teller. My slip of paper might look something like this:
  - $100s - 3
  - $50s - 2
  - $20s - 20
  - $10s - 20
  - $5s - 10
- I write a check made out to "cash" with the total amount of money I need to withdraw from our checking account.
- I do this cash withdrawal from our bank two times per month based on pay periods: the 1st and the 15th of each month.
- Once I have withdrawn the cash from the bank, I bring it home. I then open up our safe, grab our envelope system, and separate all this money into the various envelope categories.
- My wife and I take money from the envelopes when we need to go to the store, out to eat, etc.
- Any extra, unspent money from these trips goes back into the appropriate envelopes.
- During the month, I track online banking every few days to make sure deposits and withdrawals are going according to plan. If needed, I make minor adjustments to the budget along the way.
- At the end of the month, I start the entire budgeting process again (see first bullet point above).
- On the first day of a new month, I close out the previous month's budget by comparing my budgeted amounts to what my online bank account ledger states. I double check all my numbers to make sure I entered everything correctly. I give every last dollar a "name"

so that I'm being a good manager of all the money that is flowing in and out of our family.

- If we have any "extra" budget money from the previous month, then that remaining money goes to fund our goals and priorities. These goals include financial savings, investing, home improvements, or other major purchases.

The above is an example of my budget system that I work through each month. The budget is just one system in our financial strategy. We have other procedures to deal with the other parts of the plan including saving, investing, and giving.

The more systematic processes one can create to get to the place they would like to end up, the more likely they will achieve the desired outcome. Create a systematic plan, then take action on that plan.

CHALLENGE

Have you created systems for your financial life? Do you know how you are going to end up at your desired financial destination? Are you taking action on your systematic financial plan?

Download your free worksheets that go with all the chapters of this book. Go to www.heroicpersonalfinances.com/3stepsworkbook.

LEAVE A BOOK REVIEW

You have officially made it half way through the book. Congratulations! Thank you for purchasing this book and taking the time to read it. Once you finish, I would appreciate if you went over to Amazon and wrote me a quick, honest review of what you thought of the book.

Your book review does three things: one, it helps me correct any significant errors or omissions. Since the book is self-published, there are bound to be a few mistakes here and there. Second, your feedback helps me write better books in the future. Third, the more reviews I receive, the better this book can rank in the Amazon algorithm over time.

To leave a review, go to Amazon.com. In the search bar, type "Heroic Personal Finances: 3 Steps to Become A Money Hero." Click on the title and type in your comments.

Thanks in advance for leaving me a review at the end!

STEP #3
CONCENTRATE ON THE FRONT END, BUT CONTROL YOUR BACKEND

"The time making money should be greater than the time
that you are spending money."
- Sophia Amoruso[xi]

"Beware of small expenses; a small leak will sink a great ship."
- Benjamin Franklin[xii]

We live in a time in our history when real wages are either stagnant or declining for the average person. Over the last two decades, the incomes of both the middle and lower classes have either stayed steady with inflation or dropped behind it. For most of the 20th century, it was possible for a family to survive and thrive on one income. The 21st century has been a different story. With increasing inflation, especially in the area of healthcare costs, more and more families have been forced into a new paradigm. Either both parents need to work full-time jobs, or a combination of different jobs to survive and thrive with their finances.

There are a variety of reasons why real income for the lower and middle classes has fallen off over the last few decades. Because we live in such a polarized political climate, the wealthy take the brunt of the attack for much of the financial challenges of today.

Yes, the upper class have gotten richer while the middle and lower classes have gotten poorer. But, I do not believe this is due to the wealthy going out and stealing money from poor people. Sure, there are a few cases of evil rich white guys doing illegal stuff that is taking people for a ride. For the most part, though, the rich are getting richer because they know how to create more money.

Gasp! Larry, please say it isn't so. I thought the money fairy and evil white guys were colluding together to take everybody else's money away!

(Yes, I have the gift of cynicism.)

The reality is this: wealthy people know how to generate more and more income. This knowledge is how they got wealthy in the first place. The more money you bring in allows you to send it back out in investing and business creation to generate even more money. At the end of the day, it's not that complicated. But, it does take time, knowledge, and application of that knowledge to get to that next level of wealth.

Wealthy people also know how to shield and protect large portions of their income from the government. As a percentage, they pay less in taxes than most. This tax savings, of course, irritates many on one side of the political spectrum.

In my opinion, the media and politicians would be better off to quit demonizing all wealthy people. Instead, I believe we should praise them for their insight, knowledge, and resourcefulness. We should interview them on how they have achieved what they have achieved. We should copy them on how to go to the next level in our finances.

The reality is that there are already millions of books, classes, podcasts, and videos available out there today that show people how to handle money. They teach us how to generate more income, how to save money, how to spend money, and how to invest money. We have a fire hose of information available on our smart phones, 24 hours a day, seven days a week. The responsibility is ours to get off the Twitter machine and Fakebook and dig into a storehouse of wealth knowledge that is already at our fingertips.

If you want to be wealthy over the long haul, then you have to focus on the front end. You have to figure out how to generate money. You have to figure out how to invest more money that will make more money. And, you also have to control the money that's going out the back door on spending and taxes.

CHAPTER 9
YOU, INC.

Whether you realize it or not, you are in business for yourself. It doesn't matter whether you work for yourself or somebody else. We would all be wise to think of ourselves as individual corporations - "You, Inc."

When people are in business for themselves, how do they think? What are their priorities? If I could condense all ideas down to one answer, it would be this: to deliver a product or service that creates a profit.

For example, Apple, Inc. creates beautiful products that are in high demand from their customers. The company sells millions of their products and makes billions of dollars as a result. As another example, your local cable company sells services such as TV, internet, and phone. For a monthly fee, you receive regular service for these items. Millions of people subscribe to these services, and the cable companies make billions of dollars providing these services.

If you work for yourself, you need to determine what exactly is bringing in the cash flow to feed yourself and your family. Are you selling a product or service? Are you selling enough of your product or service to create enough cash flow?

If you work for somebody else, what do you contribute that is helping your company produce a profit? Maybe you help design the products or services your business sells. Or, perhaps, you create the systems in the background that keeps the company running smoothly so it can sell more goods and services. There can be many different answers to this question. A word of advice for those who work for someone else: figure out your best financial contribution to the company and double down on that contribution. My second word of counsel is to track your personal activities and outcomes for both you and your workplace. You can see what is working best for your individual output, plus you have a record to point back to so you can show your direct supervisor.

To maximize your income potential at work, again, this is where you have to think in terms of being in business for yourself. You need to expand and grow your personal capacity in your work environment. Investing in education and training will take a person further in their careers as they believe they can go. This investment into personal growth may even take a person into another career or area of expertise. I'm not talking about spending a bunch of money to go back to college and finish another degree, either. I'm talking about educational investment through reading relevant books, magazines, and blogs. Or, it can be as simple as listening to audio books, training programs, podcasts, or attending conferences. Allow other leaders in the industry to be mentors! There are many ways to invest in one's self that will cost more in time than in money.

Whether you work for yourself or someone else, you have to have the producer mindset, not a consumer one if you want to succeed with money. A consumer is one who takes more than they make. They take more time, food, money, and more. They walk around with an attitude of "what's in it for me?" The majority of people would seem to have a consumer mindset. We can see this mindset reflected in the levels of personal debt in the average household. A producer creates more than they consume. There's always plenty leftover for everyone to enjoy.

We need more people walking around with a producer mindset. Individuals who understand the importance of creating value for others and giving back. Those who have this type of mentality end up living a wealthier life as a result.

If you've never thought that way before when it comes to your career, there's no better time to start than right now. You have to take ownership of the fact that you are the CEO of You, Inc. If you work for someone else, maximize your career earning potential. Develop your producer mindset, creating more value for those you serve.

If there's little to no room for growth and advancement in your career field, then it may be time to consider a change. Or, maximize your career potential to the best of your ability and create a side hustle to generate as much extra income as time and energy will allow.

CHAPTER 10
ABUNDANCE VERSUS LACK

My youngest two daughters are four and two years old at the time I am writing this book. They are also in the middle of binge-watching their current favorite movie, *Finding Dory*. I swear the other day we watched this film a total of three times in the course of an afternoon!

If you are somewhat familiar with the movie and characters, you may recall that there are several scenes focused on a beluga whale named Bailey. Bailey hurt his head and has difficulty using echolocation to locate other characters in pipes, through walls, and so on. In the movie, they describe echolocation as "the world's most powerful pair of glasses." When Bailey finally figures out how to "turn on" his beautiful gift of echolocation, he cries out "my life's a rainbow!" He can now see a different world than those around him. He has a view filled with more hope and possibility than he did before.

The same goes with money. There are two ways of looking at the financial world. The first way of viewing the world is through a scarcity viewpoint. There are not enough resources available to all of us. You need to "grab all you can and can all you get as soon as you can!" The second way is to see the abundance of wealth and resources that are flowing all around us every day. This abundance mindset is, of course, a more powerful way in which to the view the world.

Yes, at some level our resources are finite. We can't just sit at home, printing up a bunch of money to do whatever we want. We'll let the federal government handle that department! But, I do believe we have to be careful on how we view the resources that are within reach. If you have the knowledge and determination on how to access these resources, then you will have everything you need, when you need it.

But, when I feel I don't have the necessary resources to "do life" at the level I would like to; when I don't have the money to buy the house or car that I "think" I need to buy; when I don't think I have the necessary resources to run my business or do my job at the level I believe it needs to do done, I often fall into an attitude of lack.

An attitude of scarcity in today's society is completely understandable. Politicians have put their unique spin on the American capitalistic economic system. They have conditioned people about the "haves" and the "have-nots." The world labels the wealthy as "cheaters" who don't deserve what they have. Some politicians have gone so far as stating that the government should redistribute the wealth of the top 20 percent to the poorer 80 percent of people. They want the government to operate as a modern day Robin Hood on a massive societal scale.

An abundance mindset looks at the world from a different viewpoint, though. It's like putting on a different set of glasses when viewing the economic world. Tremendous wealth is evident, and amazing possibilities abound. Instead of being jealous of the wealthy for tapping into abundance, celebrate their genius and hard work. You want to know how they achieved what they have accomplished.

Have you ever noticed how the less financially resourced in the world behave about money? They're "tight" with whatever they have. They have a closed-fist mentality with their money. What's also true, though, is money can't flow into that closed hand either.

In an open-handed approach with money, some money can escape—but even more, flows back in. Work to remain open to a world of financial possibilities. The abundance mentality looks at the world as a world of infinite possibilities, not a world of lack and limited choices.

This prosperity approach doesn't mean being wild and free with money, throwing it around and hoping for the best. No, a monthly budget that assigns every dollar a place is still important. The abundance mindset plugs financial leaks—such as taxes and other expenses—in a family's finances. We don't want to be wasteful with what we have.

The main idea I want readers to come away with from this section is that we live in a world of abundance, even in a struggling economy. Wealth surrounds us, flowing all around us every day. Our job is to tap into this financial flow of money and multiply these resources.

The poor dwell on thoughts of lack and need, while the wealthy focus on abundance and endless possibilities. Making the mental shift from thinking about abundance instead of scarcity will open up a whole new world of financial opportunities.

CHAPTER 11
THE THREE TYPES OF INCOME

People generate income in at least one of three ways. The wealthy tend to have multiple revenue streams and make money in all three forms. When you focus on your financial front end, see if you can come up with creative ways to generate more income through these three revenue sources.

First, there is linear income. A person is paid to show up to work and perform a variety of tasks—with a paycheck for work at a predetermined time. When the employee stops working, except for in the case of paid time off, they stop receiving an income. The majority of people have a least one (sometimes more) source of linear income. In a nutshell, the employee shows up for work, performs tasks for a set amount of time, and the workplace pays them for their time on the job. This type of work can range from the hamburger flipper at the local burger shack all the way up to the brain surgeon in the operating room. The pay scales are completely different, but the concept is the same. A company pays people to be on location to perform a particular task. Of course, there are various levels of linear work, where a person may be able to work less but enjoy a bigger payout at the end. For the sake of simplicity, though, I won't chase down the multitude of ways to earn linear income.

The second type of income is passive income. Passive income is revenue generated from money working for a person via investments. Money may be in CDs, money market accounts, higher-yield savings accounts, various types of bonds, and then, of course, the stock exchange. Real estate investing could be in this mix as well. If all the markets are behaving, passive investment income is significant. But, if one is riding the stock market roller coaster, passive income is not so much fun. Passive income usually requires little extra work depending on the investment strategy. The person earns money, and then they put the money to work. A passive income strategy is great for building retirement savings, but not always the best way to support a family, unless there are millions of dollars at work.

The third and perhaps most interesting type of income is residual income. The definition of residual income is income that continues to be generated after initial effort has been expended. Do the work once, and then receive income from that work spread out over time. Types of residual income would include the following: affiliate marketing, subscription services, book sales, drop ship websites, pay-per-click online ads, and vending machines. Pat Flynn from SmartPassiveIncome.com is an example of someone who has created residual income products that provide well for his family. Pat's journey to residual income all started from a layoff from his architecture job in 2008. He then created a website to help himself pass an architecture industry exam called the LEED exam. Little did Pat know that his little website was generating thousands of visits per day. People loved his content and expressed their desire for an eBook of his LEED material. This feedback from website visitors is when the "lights came on" for Pat. He created the eBook, and within the first month of being for sale, he made $7,008.55! Since that time, Pat has not turned back. He has created even more residual streams of income. In 2014, he earned almost $1,000,000 in revenue from all his residual/passive income streams.

Residual income should be the ultimate goal when focusing on the front end of your finances—creating multiple streams of income and no longer being dependent on one or two linear revenue sources. When you have this multiple streams of income mindset, you are playing the money game in offense mode versus defense mode.

Many of us have the tendency to play our money game on defense. We are trying not to lose any money. But, we're so focused on not losing any money, we forget that we also need to spend more time on the offense side of money if we're going to win in the end. Have a great defensive money game, but don't forget to stay on offense for the majority of your money game. Focus on generating more and more income through these three types - linear, passive, and residual.

CHAPTER 12
LONG-TERM FINANCIAL PLANNING

Part of concentrating on the front end of your personal finances is taking the long view of how you want to end your financial journey. Long-term financial planning is necessary to accomplish that long view.

In the previous chapter, I mentioned the second type of income - passive income. This kind of revenue is your money generating, even more, money. The end goal should be a big enough pile of money accumulated through savings and investing that these funds are making enough money in interest payments to sustain at least your current lifestyle level and more.

And, if you can combine the second and third types of income - passive and residual - then you will be in an excellent position to not need to punch a time clock for the rest of your life. You will have systems in place that are generating a flow of money into your life for the rest of your life. Plus, you will have a legacy to hand down to future generations.

Again, this goes all the way back to "the vision thing" back in Step #1. Begin with the end in mind. In a perfect world, when do you want to retire? What lifestyle do you want to have the capacity to live when you reach that age? Have you calculated how much money you would need to generate in passive and residual income to be able to live that lifestyle?

The sooner you can get all passive and residual money streams into place, working hard for you for the next few decades, the wealthier you will be.

Alright, so let's cut to the chase. Let's get more practical instead of talking theory here. What systems could one put into place as soon as possible for long term financial planning? There are many possibilities. Based on my knowledge and experience, I would say focus on the following:

In the area of passive income, you need to be a high capacity saver and investor. Automate your savings and investing with the most money you can put away each month. Diversify your savings and investing. You can auto draft a percentage of your income into a "high yield" savings account each month. I place "high yield" in quotes because, at the time of this writing, high yield equals one percent. Not great returns for passive income, but it's handy to have some liquid cash for emergencies. One could also setup an investment grade whole life insurance policy to create a "bank" or pool of money for personal borrowing or investment purposes. These life policies are also known as the Infinite Banking Concept (IBC). I won't take the time to explain an IBC here in this book. Check out the following website for more information: https://infinitebanking.org/about/.

One can maximize returns in their retirement accounts such as IRAs and 401(k)s to put money to work as effectively and efficiently as possible. Another potential money investing strategy: save money in a "high yield" savings account during bull stock markets, waiting out the market for the next bear market. When the market appears to have bottomed out, then invest all your investment savings into quality, trophy asset companies and ride the market back up to new record levels. Peer-to-peer lending websites such as Prosper and Lending Club are another place to put money to work.

Residual income is the "holy grail" of money generation. If one can create businesses with products and services, and be paid multiple times over and over for years after doing the work once, they are on track to real wealth. Once one can separate their personal time out of the money equation, this is where money starts working in exponential ways. Is it difficult? Yes, most definitely. But, if one can achieve success in residual income, the rewards are fantastic.

Also in the area of residual income, one can pursue investment real estate, residential or commercial. The one thing investors have to watch out for is making sure to buy their real estate at a discount so that the property can cash flow from the start.

As you get healthy in your personal finances through a vision and decision and by creating a plan and taking action, be sure to think about how you can generate more income with less time effort over the long term. In this way, your retirement years shouldn't be filled with as much stress and doubt if you have set up income streams for a lifetime.

CHAPTER 13
THE 10-10-80 RULE

In Chapters 9-12, we focused on the importance of getting more income flowing through the front door. Now, let's turn our attention to controlling the money that is going out the back door. Several years ago, I heard about a simple personal finance system called the 10-10-80 Rule. Here's the basic plan:

- Give 10%
- Save 10%
- Spend 80%

If you're not into doing complex budget spreadsheets, this simple 10-10-80 money breakdown is a great starting point to learn how to handle your personal finances.

First, we begin with giving away 10% of our income. In the church world, we call this a tithe, but it doesn't matter if you're a church goer or not. There are many secularists and non-church people who regularly give to a variety of favorite causes and charities. Now, you may be asking yourself, "Larry, why in the world would I just give 10% right off the top of my income. That seems a little strange if I should be managing my money wisely? Maybe I would be better off investing that 10% instead of giving it away?"

These are great questions to ask. I agree that giving away 10% of your money off the top seems counterintuitive to becoming a hero with your money. But, I have also learned from personal experience and the experience of others that giving back has several positive effects on both you and your money. It makes you more generous, kind, and caring to those who are in need around you every day. It causes you to live with an open-handed approach to life. The great thing about living life with an open hand instead of a closed fist is that not only can money flow out of that open hand, but also more money can flow back into your life. We become conduits of money through living a generous lifestyle. As I learn to be a more generous person, I become a wealthier person. These principles are all interconnected. Being a giver can also cause you to become a more

43

disciplined person. If I have decided I'm going to give 10% of my money away, then I have to be a little more structured and disciplined with the remaining 90%.

Second, we save at least 10% of our income. Again, having this regular savings practice along with our giving practice helps us to become more disciplined with what we have flowing into our lives. We should be saving money in regular bank savings accounts for a rainy day fund. We should save money into "sinking funds" when we are trying to save money each month for major purchases such as large appliances, cars, and home repairs. And yes, we should be investing part of our money, putting it away for our eventual retirement which we discussed in the previous chapter.

Third, we have 80% remaining to pay for our everyday expenses. Because we have planned to give away 10% as well as save 10% of our money, we have to discipline ourselves enough to live on the remaining 80%. To do this, though, one needs at least a simple cashflow plan of rent, mortgage, bills, and other expenses that one pays out each month. An excellent way to figure out what is going out the back door of your finances, purpose ahead of time that over at least a time span of one or two months that you are going to save every bill or receipt and total them up at the end of the month. Anytime you go out to eat, keep the receipt. Any time you put gas in your car, save the receipt. Any time you make a run to the grocery store, keep the receipt. With all your utility bills, do the same.

Over the course of a few weeks, you should have a pretty good idea of where your money is going. Some of these expenses are going to be out of your control. You will need to plan for them and spend the money. Other expenses, though, will be more discretionary spending that you can control. If your financial situation is challenging, then do your best to cut what you can cut. Remember that the purpose of cutting back in certain areas is about funding your financial vision that we talked about back in Step #1.

To save money, maybe you can eat out less and eat at home more. Perhaps you can use coupons when you go to the grocery store. Maybe you can save on gas money by making fewer trips and consolidating the various errands you run each week. There are a variety ways you can tweak your money outgo to be more efficient and accomplish more.

CHAPTER 14
DEBT AND SAVINGS

One way we can be more efficient and effective with our money is to get out of consumer debt as fast as possible. Debt is the biggest way in which people are losing hundreds, even thousands of dollars out the back door of their personal finances each month. If they fix this part of their personal finances as soon as possible, they will make more and more money over time.

One of the biggest ways to save money today is through not paying revolving credit on credit cards. When credit card interest averages 18-21% interest each month and you only pay the minimum payment, you see money fly out the back door of your finances. You could make a significant financial turnaround by paying off these major interest debt payments as soon as possible.

What about car loans? Even though most car payments have fixed payments with lower interest rates, you still have money flying out of your back pocket and into your bank CEO's golden parachute because of vehicle depreciation. The depreciation on a brand new car is frightening. The average loss rates look like this: let's say you financed a new car at $25,000. Within one year of owning that vehicle, you would have lost, on average, $3,750 which is 15% of the value of the car. And then in 4 years, you would lose on average $9,647, which is around 38% of the value. The typical car loan percentage rate is around 4-5% at the time of this writing. So, even though you're paying a low rate of interest to buy a new car, you're paying way more than that due to the depreciation factor on vehicles.

The same applies to any other consumer personal debt such as payday loans, title loans, IRS debt, medical bills, home equity loans, and student loans. The faster you can cut these debt payments from your life, the sooner you can be saving and investing money. You will move your focus from the backend of your finances to your front end.

So how do we pay these debts off as soon as possible? While concentrating on the front end of your finances, trying to get as much extra income in the front door as fast as possible through your regular income and side hustles, you need to come up with a strategic plan to quickly and efficiently pay off all your debt.

There are a couple of effective debt repayment methods that many financial experts recommend and use: the debt avalanche and the debt snowball methods.

In the debt avalanche method, you list all your debts based on the current interest rate, starting with the debt with the highest rate. So, for the sake of example, let's say you have a car loan at 4.67% with a remaining balance of $4,000, a student loan at 7.21% for $25,000, and a credit card at 18.99% for $15,000. The debt avalanche method would have you order these for accelerated payoff by the interest rate. Put the credit card first on the list, followed by the student loan, and finally end with the car loan. The line of thinking of this method is that the higher the interest rate, the more money you are losing every month based on the interest rate. You will save more money over time with this method. The one challenge with this approach can be when the higher interest rate debts are the largest debts. You have less disposable income on the front end to pay these higher interest rate debts down as fast as possible. This approach usually takes longer to cut the first couple of debts. You could lose momentum and quit trying to pay off your debt sooner than later.

In the debt snowball method, you ignore interest rates and list your debts from smallest to largest. The reason is simple. Even though you may be working on paying off debts with lower interests rates first, which makes no sense from a financial standpoint, money is all about psychology. Using this method, you will pay off the little debts a lot faster at the beginning of the process. Having these small wins taking place early on gives people a sense of success and momentum. They are more likely to stick with their plan over the long term. In this approach, early success trumps financial math, because money is more about psychology and less about the math. Now, let's go back to the three debt examples I gave above. If one were to use the debt snowball method to pay these three debts, they should place them in the following order: pay off the car first, then move on to the credit card, and finally, work on the student debt.

Focused, fast debt repayment is one of the best ways to make money and get momentum working for you in your financial life. Once you can drop these debts and get the money to stop flowing out the back door of your finances, it's a whole lot easier to save money for emergencies and create sinking funds for future purchases. Here are a few thoughts on savings.

The general rule of thumb when saving money after you have paid off all your consumer debts is to sock away three to six months worth of expense money in a money market account or the highest percentage yield you can find in an online bank. I referenced my multi-tiered savings plan back in Chapter 6, "Areas to Plan." I like using this layered savings approach to cover various types of emergencies that could arise.

Another wise move when it comes to savings is developing "sinking funds" for larger, major purchases. In today's online connected world, there are several significant banking resources out there that can assist in automatically saving part of your income in a sub-section of a savings account. Once that sub-account has the appropriate amount of money to buy whatever you may be saving for, you can close that down and withdraw the money to make the purchase. I have used this method for saving my first major emergency fund as well as for a downpayment on our house. "Smartypig" is the banking tool I used to set-up these sub-accounts. They call these savings goals, and they have many useful features to assist with your sinking fund savings strategy. Check out their website at https://www.smartypig.com.

There are other banks out there that offer similar options when it comes to setting up sub-accounts for savings, Check out Capital One 360 at https://www.capitalone.com/savings-accounts/online-savings-account/. Another bank to look at for sub-accounts is Ally Financial at https://www.ally.com/savings-accounts/multiple-savings-accounts/.

One of the best personal finance strategies to help with both the income and outgo in your money plan is to get out of all consumer debt as fast as possible, followed by a strategic, automated savings plan. I credit this for being the "secret sauce" for helping me become a money hero. The path to paying off debt and saving money happens through utilizing budgets, cash flow plans, and strategic money management.

CHAPTER 15
BUDGETS AND CASH FLOW PLANNING

If you want to become a superhero with money, then you have to create various systems to control the money that's going out the back door in the form of spending. Having a budget is the number one tool to become that money hero.

Most people don't like to plan their personal finances. They think it's too restrictive and won't allow them to live the life they want. They believe that it takes too much time, and they won't be able to stick with their plan for more than a month or two. They give up and go back to their usual lack of a plan and bad spending habits. If people would just give the budgeting process some time, say four to six months, then they would find that it becomes easier the longer they do it. When one gets used to the budgeting process, it takes less and less time. Having a personal budget in place can be a freeing, empowering experience over time.

Going back to my analogy of being in business for yourself, You, Inc., in Chapter 9, let me ask the following question. What legitimate business would operate without a spending plan? If that company wants to succeed, then they need to have some mechanism in place to curb spending and maximize their business income. A business without a cash flow plan will soon be out of business. If a company put you in charge of their finances and you didn't produce an annual budget with monthly targets, then you would soon find yourself without a job!

You as an individual are in business for yourself, whether you acknowledge that fact or not. You have the power to succeed with money, through using an organized cash flow plan.

How does one go through the process of setting up a budget? Great question! I'm glad you asked. If starting from scratch, here would be my recommendation to get the process rolling.

First, take some time, perhaps two to four weeks, to get your bearings on what you may spend in a given month if you are prone to not paying attention to your spending. Gather up all your bills in a given month: utility bills, credit card statements, rent or mortgage payments, bank statements, and checkbooks. Also, track your everyday spending by keeping every receipt you get. And, if you aren't offered a receipt for your spending, then be sure to ask for one! If you go to the coffee shop, get a receipt. If you go out to lunch with friends, keep your receipt. When you get gas for your car, then print off the receipt at the pump. When you go to the grocery store for food, keep the receipt. Anytime you spend money whether it's cash, debit, or credit card, be sure to ask for and keep the receipt. Store these in a safe place that you can come back to in a few weeks.

After gathering up your regular monthly bills and at least a couple of weeks worth of daily spending receipts, take some time to analyze where your money is going. Take out a piece of paper, and start jotting down some basic numbers. Start with your regular bills that you must pay, no matter what: rent, mortgage, utilities, and so on. Next, move into the categories of more discretionary spending: food, clothing, and other impulse purchases. Separate your receipts into these various categories, add them up, and estimate what you spend in a given month. For example, you figure that you're spending $300/month eating out at restaurants. Perhaps, you discover that you spend approximately $200/month in gas purchases at the pump. Right now, you don't need to be exact. Just get some estimates put together and write them down.

Now that you have a better idea of where your money is going in a given month, now is the time to start the process of a formal budget cash flow plan. There are several ways you can go about this, from simple to complex. I will say from the outset, though, the easier you can make your plan from month to month, the greater chance you will stick with the plan.

You could start with the low-tech approach of a legal pad of paper and a pen. At the top of the page, list out all your sources of income and add those up: your income, spouse's income, gifts, second jobs, social security payments, and so on. Next, put giving as the first thing you do with your money as I mentioned back in Chapter 6. After giving, make sure you have accounted for all your tax money to payout, especially if you need to pay quarterly estimated filings or other local taxes. Finally, be certain to account for all your monthly expenses: mortgage, rent, utilities, insurances, groceries, eating out, savings, investing, car payments, credit card payments and so on.

Once you have all your bills estimated and written down, total up all your giving, any taxes, and monthly expenses. Take this total and subtract from your total income. The goal here is to equal zero. This process is known as zero-based budgeting. We are telling every dollar we have coming through the front door what to do. If you have "leftover" money after you subtract expenses from income, then you need to give that extra money something to do. You may need the excess cash flow to help pay down some debt. Or, perhaps you need to put the extra money in savings for a rainy day. The key is to have a financial plan and use excess cash flow to work your plan.

What if the opposite is the case, though? If instead of extra money at the end of your budget process, you are in negative numbers. You are overspending your income. What now? You will need to go back through your estimated budget plan and see if you can cut some areas that you can fund at a later date. Potential areas in which you can cut is called discretionary spending. Budget categories such as clothing, dining out, entertainment, and perhaps some gas or grocery money would fall under discretionary spending. Cut where you can, and, again, try to get your budget to equal zero when you subtract your expenses from your income.

Since many costs are similar from month to month, it gets pretty old doing this longhand on a yellow legal pad. It's a lot easier and faster to have a reproducible electronic spreadsheet that you can alter each month. I use an Excel budget spreadsheet, so I don't have to start over all the time. For my readers, I have made a monthly estimated budget Excel spreadsheet available for free that you can download. Go to www.heroicpersonalfinances.com/freebudgetform to request your copy via email.

Finally, there are also a few online tools available if you don't want to use spreadsheets or legal pads. Check out the online budget tool and app created by the Ramsey Solutions team at https://www.everydollar.com. You can also use the Mint website and app at https://www.mint.com. Personal Capital may be another option at https://www.personalcapital.com. There are several choices available. Google search "best online budget tools" and see what pops up.

Once you have your budget set up and ready to roll, the next system you need to set in place is deciding how you will pay your bills and expenses. We will cover this topic in the next chapter.

CHAPTER 16
MONEY MANAGEMENT

In Chapter 8, we discussed the importance of systems. The most successful, disciplined people put systems in place to keep them successful and disciplined.

Now that we have a cash flow spending plan in place from the last chapter let's dig a little deeper into long term money management strategies that will help us continue being a money hero.

First, you need to determine how you will pay your regular ongoing monthly bills. Will you hand write checks and lick stamps and envelopes on a "bills night" once a month? In today's culture, paying bills the old fashioned way is unnecessary. You could spend that time more efficiently elsewhere. My recommendation is to use bill automation. I set this up years ago. Best thing I ever did in my personal finances. I either called companies or went to their websites and setup auto-drafts for all our regular expenses from mortgage payments, utility bills, college loans, credit card bills, and insurance payments. Our bills are automatically paid from our checking account each month. No more bills night or envelope licking! All I do is check our bank account online every few days to make sure all the appropriate bills and amounts are paid. Just remember to account in your budget for bills that vary month to month.

Second, after you have determined the budget categories that will be paid via auto draft, the next step is to determine which expenses you will pay by debit and credit cards. For example, my wife and I pay for gas at the pump with our credit or debit cards. I know some people who live on tighter budgets may use cash. Fortunately for us, we have a bit more flexibility in our budget. Plus, because the price of gas fluctuates from week to week and we like the convenience of paying at the pump so we can fill our tanks to the top, using our credit or debit cards makes more sense for us. I keep tabs on our gas purchases each month and account for them in our budget.

Third, the final layer of payment deals with those items that you may want to pay for in cash. In today's world, many people don't even like to carry around cash with them. Paying with cash, though, is one of the best ways to stay on track with your budget, especially variable expenses that could get out of control using debit and credit cards. It's a well-known, researched fact that people tend to spend more when paying with cards versus cash. In our family, we use the envelope system to pay cash for the following categories in our budget: grocery money, dining out, blow money, and babysitters. I budget a set amount for each category. I then determine which monetary denominations I need for each section. For example, every two weeks, I might budget $100 for dining out. I would then decide that we should get three $20 bills, three $10 bills, and two $5 bills to put in our dining out envelope. I will figure out these money denominations for all our envelopes in our envelope system, add up all the various denominations and write that down on a slip of paper. I then write a check to "cash" for the total amount and go to the bank to cash my check in those various denominations. I do this twice a month, at each pay period on the 1st and 15th of every month.

We have worked this multi-layered money management system for years. I attribute the majority of whatever success we have had with money to utilizing this system. This format helped me and my family pay off approximately $130,000 worth of debt, put a healthy downpayment on a new house, and pay cash for two reliable used vehicles. Automate what you can. Use credit or debit cards when it makes sense to do so. Finally, use cash to reign in your spending in areas that tempt you to overspend.

In the next chapter, we will look at a few more systems to help you and your family with your financial organization.

CHAPTER 17
FINANCIAL ORGANIZATION
AND ASSET PROTECTION

If you want to be successful in personal finances, then you need to take some time on the front end to get organized. Then you need to take some time every few months to stay organized over the long haul. Whenever you work on your financial budget at the beginning and end of the month, this may be a good time to take a quick assessment of your finances. Figure out what you need to stay organized and on top of your financial vision and systems.

One area of financial organization you want to stay on top of is your credit score. I used to drink the Kool-aid from one finance expert when it came to credit ratings. As a result of listening to him, I ended up cutting up all my credit cards, paid off all my consumer debts, and then used online banking, debit cards, checks, and cash for all my purchases for seven years. I had gone so long without using credit that I "fell off the grid" in the credit reporting world. FICO® couldn't calculate my score, almost as if I was deceased! This adherence to no credit on my part ended up causing my wife and I some concern when we were preparing to buy a home a couple of years ago. I was talking to my real estate agent over lunch about my concerns, and he suggested that I open up one or two credit cards in my name to see if I could get my credit score to return in a few months. I took his advice, and within four or five months, my credit score returned. My wife and I were able to get great terms on a mortgage loan because we both have excellent credit scores.

I know many people struggle with consumer debt. They can't keep a credit card in their wallet because they will end up in debt up to their eyeballs before they know what happened to them. If you're that type of money personality, then you need to cut up all your credit cards and never use them again. Or, perhaps one could have a few automated expenses on one card to keep the card active for credit reporting purposes. Then, you could freeze the card in a block of ice inside your freezer or put it in a safe deposit box at your bank, so you won't be tempted to use it.

When I received my two cards to re-establish my credit score, I went online as soon as they arrived in the mail and put them on auto payment from our checking account each month. I never want to hold a balance and get socked with high-interest rate charges. I know this makes me a "deadbeat" to my two credit card companies, but I'm not using their cards to make them money. I'm using them to keep my credit score active and as high as possible for home buying purposes.

You may be asking the question about how to stay on top of your credit score. There are several different ways to check your number. Some of these methods cost money, which is a total waste of money in my opinion. The free and easy way for me to watch my number has been through my Mint app that I mentioned back in Chapter 15. Also, one of my credit cards tracks my FICO® score for free. Whenever I log into my account with this particular bank, I can see my credit score right on the home page.

The second area of your financial organization that you want to keep track of similar to credit scores is your credit report. It would be a wise move to check your credit report for errors and potential ID theft every four months. You can do this for free on the website annualcreditreport.com. If you only download a single, different report from one of the three credit reporting agencies (Equifax, Experian, or TransUnion) every four months, then you can get it for free. My suggestion is to set up an annual reminder in your phone calendar for all three reporting agencies. On April 1 of each year, have your calendar remind you to check your Equifax report. On August 1 of each year, have your calendar alert you to check your Experian report. Finally, on December 1 of each year, set a reminder to check your TransUnion report.

The third area of financial organization is keeping all relevant information together in one place. This information would include the following: bank accounts, credit cards, all your insurance carriers and info (health, home, auto, life, disability, etc), investing accounts, location of critical paperwork, any online accounts someone may need access to if you aren't here, social media account login information, personal login information for computers, tablets, phones, business account(s) information if you own your own business(es). If you are single, you may want to type everything out on a single sheet of paper, put in a safe place, and tell a trusted family member or friend how to access the information. If married, you could keep both an electronic version and paper version of all the above information, then place it in a safe location and let your spouse know. For an electronic copy of this information, I like using a note in my Evernote app that can be accessed on all our computers and portable electronic devices. Anytime I update all this valuable information, I print off a new paper copy and place it in a safe location that my wife knows about, just in case something happens to me. Nothing says "I love you" more to your loved ones than preparing them for when you will be gone, especially if you are the "money person" in your family.

Speaking of safe places to store valuables and important paperwork, there are a couple of ways to go about this. One, you can pay a monthly fee and get a safe deposit box at your bank. The main drawback to safe deposit boxes is that you can only access these during bank hours. In an emergency situation in the middle of the night when you need access to critical documents or other articles stored there, you won't be able to get what you need.

Two, you can buy a well-built safe and place it in a hidden location in your home. The great news about a safe in your home is access 24 hours a day, seven days a week. The bad news is that you could be robbed of valuable articles and financial information. My opinion is that in home safes are the way to go, but whatever method of storage works for you and your family.

The purpose of insurance is asset protection. One bad accident or one horrible lawsuit later, you could be cleaned out of all your significant assets - your house, cars, savings, and investments. Everything could be completely taken away to settle a tax bill or a court case. You want to be sure you have the best quality insurance at the right cost to cover all the major areas: health, auto, home (or renter's), life, disability, and long-term care insurance at age 55 and beyond. If you start gathering even larger amounts of assets beyond $1 million, then you might also consider umbrella policies that will provide even more asset coverage on top of all your other insurances. Don't go cheap in this area, either. You don't want to pay more than you need to, but you also want adequate coverage so that your assets don't get taken away because of one stupid mistake.

Keeping your financial life organized and protected over the long haul is important for both you and your family. Be sure to cover your financial backend, and don't procrastinate in these critical areas.

CHAPTER 18
PLUG UP YOUR TAX LEAKS

Taxes. Nobody likes them, but they are one of those necessary evils in life that everyone must deal with. They are one of the biggest drains on people's financial backend. One of the wisest moves we can make to control any money going out the back door of our personal finances is to take every legal tax deduction available. In this chapter, I'll offer some thoughts, ideas, and resources for lowering tax obligations.

Let me pause here and say that I am not a CPA, tax advisor, or financial planner. I don't play one on the Internet, either. For the most part, I'm just a regular guy with a few tax advantages than the average taxpayer who does his taxes each year with downloaded software. I am also required to pay quarterly estimated taxes instead of having taxes deducted from my paychecks. Maybe that's a good thing or a bad thing. All I know is that I feel the "pain" of paying taxes, and I'm always on the lookout for legal ways to lower my family's tax obligations.

Don't discount the importance of having an intelligent, strategic, and implemented tax strategy. A wise tax plan has the long-term potential to put tens of thousands and maybe even hundreds of thousands of dollars in a person's pocket. If doing taxes is not a personal strength, consider hiring a tax professional to help. Ask people for recommendations. Hiring the right tax person is money well worth spending, and they will save money in the long run.

Here's a good rule of thumb in dealing with taxes: use whatever tax strategies are available in a given year to reduce adjusted gross taxable income as low as possible. The goal is to move down into lower tax brackets and, of course, pay a lower percentage in taxes. Wealthy people follow this strategy. Perhaps, this is why they are wealthy?

Now, let's talk deductions to move into those lower tax brackets. Here's a listing of various deductions to be aware of when using tax software or a tax professional to determine eligibility for the deductions. The list below is not comprehensive, but I've listed the largest ones of which I'm aware. I've also separated these by category. Most on this list I found through a GoBankingRates/TaxAct online article as well as from my personal experience.

Family Deductions:

1. **Standard Deduction.** In 2014, single filers could deduct $6,200 from earned income, $12,400 for married couples filing jointly, and $9,100 for heads of households.

2. **Personal Exemptions.** You, your spouse and your kids all qualify as exemptions on your taxes unless someone else can claim them ahead of you (such as an ex-spouse, etc.). For the year 2014, you could claim $3,950 per individual.

3. **Dependent Care Flex Spending.** If you take advantage of an FSA through your workplace, you can contribute up to $5,000 pre-tax toward dependent care expenses. As long as the costs qualify, you won't be taxed on that money.

4. **Childcare Expenses.** If you don't use flex spending, you can still deduct childcare expenses on your tax forms. All deductible expenses must be necessary to keep you and your spouse employed.

Home Deductions: (You can only claim these deductions if you own your home and have a mortgage.)

1. **Mortgage Insurance Premiums Deduction.** If you itemize your taxes (and not do the EZ forms!), you may be able to deduct your PMI premiums paid on your home.

2. **Home Mortgage Interest.** If you itemize, then you can take this deduction.

3. **Mortgage Points.** If you itemize, then you can take this deduction on your primary residence.

4. **Points Paid on Home Improvement Loans.** If you itemize, then you may be able to take this deduction on points paid on a loan to improve your primary residence.

5. **Casualty, Disaster, and Theft Loss.** Any losses related to your home, items in your home, or vehicles that were not covered by insurance could be deductible.

Taxes Paid Deductions:

1. **State and Local Real Estate Taxes.** If you itemize your tax

forms, you may be able to deduct any local or state real estate taxes that you pay each year.

2. **State and Local Sales Tax.** You have the option to deduct either state and local income taxes or sales taxes. If you live in a state with no income tax, deduct sales taxes.

3. **Tax Preparation Fees.** If you paid someone to do your taxes or you purchased software to do it yourself, then you can deduct that expense on your tax form.

4. **Vehicle Registration Fees.** You may be able to deduct some vehicle registration fees based on the value of the vehicle. In my home state of Missouri, these are known as personal property taxes that we must pay each December on cars, trucks, SUV's, motorcycles, RV's, boats, and more.

5. **State Taxes Due.** If you are behind on your state taxes from a previous year, you may be eligible to deduct that money from your federal taxes.

Non-Profit Donation Deductions:

1. **Cash Donations.** If you donate $250 or more to specific charities or non-profits that are IRS approved, you should receive a year-end statement listing your contributions. If you itemize your taxes, then you can deduct these financial donations.

2. **Non-Cash Donations.** If you itemize, you can also deduct the fair market value of clothes and other household items that you donate. Be sure to keep receipts and pictures of the items that you give each year.

3. **Unreimbursed Expenses for Charity Work.** If you use your vehicle to help a charity, you can take the standard mileage deduction ($.14/mile), plus any tolls or parking expenses. Be sure to keep a mileage log and any receipts.

Education and Work Deductions:

1. **Tuition and Fees Deduction.** In the year 2014, you could deduct up to $4,000 in qualifying tuition and fees as long as you aren't claiming these expenses for another tax break.

2. **Student Loan Interest.** Any student loans you're paying on, you

can deduct up to $2,500 of interest paid on those loans in the year 2014.

3. **Job Search Expenses.** If you itemize, then there are certain costs you can deduct if you conduct a job search in your current career in a given year. Keep logs and receipts.

4. **Moving Expenses.** Similar to #3, if you have to move to take a new job position, you may be eligible to deduct certain expenses if you meet specific IRS qualifications. Again, keep good detailed logs and receipts.

5. **Military Reserves Travel Expenses.** For those who serve in the armed forces reserves and need to travel more than 100 miles from home to serve, you can deduct certain travel expenses. Keep good records.

Medical Deductions:

1. **Some Medical and Dental Expenses.** This scenario would be a somewhat unusual situation, but after you pay out certain percentages (7.5 - 10% based on age and income) on health care expenses in a given year, then you may be eligible to deduct expenses beyond those amounts.

2. **Health Savings Account (HSA) Contributions.** Not everyone can take advantage of an HSA. If you can, though, do it. Then, assuming you contribute pre-tax to your HSA, you will receive pre-tax savings on your healthcare money. HSA's are much better than FSA's because you don't have to spend all the money each year. Even if you don't use it all, you won't lose it. You can let these funds build up in your HSA account. My wife and I have had an HSA for the last four years. We use ours as an extra layer of emergency funds for medical expenses. We have experienced the financial benefits they give to the "average" family.

Business Deductions:

1. **Business Use of Your Home.** If you employ strategies to increase your income through your own small business or side hustle, I encourage you to form a business, either a Sole Proprietorship or better yet, an LLC. Carve out some space in your

home to serve as an office to take care of business, and then you can deduct certain expenses as a result. Win-win!

2. **Business Use of Your Car.** Be sure to keep good mileage logs and receipts to use this deduction.

3. **Business Travel Expenses.** Again, keep good records to take advantage of any potential tax savings.

4. **Self-Employed Health Insurance.** If you are self-employed having to buy your coverage for medical and dental, then you can deduct premiums paid for you and your family on your taxes.

Investing Deductions:

1. **Investment Fees and Expenses.** Fees paid to manage investments that generate taxable income are deductible.

2. **IRA Contributions.** In the year 2014, it was possible to deduct for IRA contributions up to $5,500 to $6,500, depending on age.

3. **Safe Deposit Box Rental Fees.** You can claim the cost if you use a safe deposit box for storing important paperwork related to your investments.

Here are some final thoughts outside of the realm of year-to-year tax deductions. When nearing retirement, around age 55, consider long-term strategies on taxes. It is best to be in a decent tax position when in retirement age and taking certain disbursements from retirement accounts. Consider what tax bracket is best once this happens. Also, keep in mind what role Social Security plays into retirement. Retirement tax planning strategies should be discussed with a professional who could help a retired person save a lot of money. Talk with people who have already gone through the process of maximizing their tax situation for retirement planning. Find out what tax professionals they have used. Never pay more to the government than should be paid!

CHALLENGE

Are you generating ideas to bring more money into the "front door" of your personal finances? Do you have a hobby you can turn into a "side hustle" to generate extra income? Do you have some ideas on how you can create some residual and passive revenue streams?

Are you debt free? Do you have money saved in bank accounts? Do you have a monthly cash flow plan? Are your personal finances organized?

Download your free worksheets that go with all the chapters of this book. Go to www.heroicpersonalfinances.com/3stepsworkbook.

CHAPTER 19
CONCLUSION: TAKE A FINANCIAL HEALTH DAY

Several years ago, a friend and I were joking around about his taking "mental health days" at work. He told me that he would take these days off from time to time when he was stressed out, tired, and needed to recharge his physical "batteries."

In a somewhat similar way, I found myself taking time off occasionally to do what I called "financial health days." Approximately two or three times a year, I would take paid time off to take care of those important financial life details that seem to pile up that we never make time to follow through on. These money details could include setting financial goals, opening a new bank account, setting up auto payment on utility bills, reorganizing personal financial files, establishing some new investment accounts, and more. Every time I have taken a financial health day, I've always felt a sense of accomplishment when the day was over. I have been able to cross several items off my personal finance to-do list as well as save a bunch of money and time in the process. Taking these financial days was definitely worth my time and energy.

In this book, I have laid out several personal finance ideas and strategies for consideration. Ideas and theories are great on paper, but they don't do anything unless one implements them.

So, may I make a suggestion? What if you went through this book a second time and highlighted the areas where you feel the need to action? And then, what if you take that final step of action on those areas that could make you the hero of your money story?

My recommendation would be to create your list of action items, schedule a financial health day to be held within the next couple of weeks, and then take massive action on your special money day. I know you'll be glad you did!

To assist you with your action plan and financial health day, I have put together a short downloadable workbook to help you walk through these three steps to become the hero of your money. Go to: www.heroicpersonalfinances.com/3stepsworkbook to get your copy delivered by email.

LEAVE A BOOK REVIEW

Thank you so much for taking the time to read this book. If you found value with what you read, I would appreciate if you went over to Amazon and wrote me a quick, honest review of what you thought of the book.

Your book review does three things: one, it helps me correct any significant errors or omissions. Since the book is self-published, there are bound to be a few mistakes here and there. Second, your feedback helps me write better books in the future. Third, the more reviews I receive, the better this book can rank in the Amazon algorithm over time.

To leave a review, go to Amazon.com. In the search bar, type "Heroic Personal Finances: 3 Steps to Become A Money Hero." Click on the title and type in your comments.

Thanks in advance for leaving me a review!

OTHER BOOKS BY LARRY JONES

**Heroic Personal Finances for Christians:
Accelerating Past Average With Your Money Plan**

Are you a Christian who has gone through church small group money classes such as Crown Financial or Financial Peace University™? If so, have you felt like important money management strategies are missing from their content?

Have you ever wondered if there is more to financial investing than a four-part, 25% in growth stock mutual funds approach? Have you ever questioned if a focus on stock market investing, college savings, and paying off the home early can actually create long-term wealth? Have you ever had the thought that maybe certain financial experts have "painted themselves into a corner" when it comes to advanced money management practices?

In this book, Larry draws on the rich insights of a variety of experts such as Tim Ferriss, Robert Kiyosaki, Andy Stanley, Robert Morris, Tony Robbins, Stephen Covey, Napoleon Hill, Michael Hyatt, R. Nelson Nash, and Dave Ramsey.

Using valuable "nuggets" of financial wisdom from these renowned experts, Generosity Pastor Larry Jones dug himself out of debt TWICE for a total of $130,000 in debt repayment over nine years. And in the middle of this financial mess, he survived a difficult divorce while staying faithful to his calling to ministry. This book weaves his personal story along with what he learned through a ten-year period of his life.

In *Heroic Personal Finances for Christians*, Pastor Larry inspires you to consider this highly researched Christian, personal finance journey. This book will:

- Lay a solid foundation for your money plan.
- Equip you with strategic action steps for a disciplined life.
- Give a multi-step approach to grow in the area of generosity.
- Focus on "habit stacking" and wealthy morning rituals.
- Explain the concept of the "investment pyramid."
- Encourage an 80/20 (Pareto Principle) focus in your work habits.
- Supply a highly actionable emergency preparedness plan.
- Remind you to "plug up" any tax leaks.
- Develop ideas for creating multiple streams of income.
- Coach you on several strategies to put your money to work.

"Really astounded by the level of depth and detail in this book. Extremely well written and compelling. This is a book that NEEDED to be written. For anyone who has followed and believed in the Biblical money advice of Dave Ramsey, this book delivers the next level. The book is written from a stronger Christian perspective than Dave's books, so know that from the start. But it is also written from a more holistic perspective. While Dave tends to segregate money and earning from home life, Larry reconnects the two. And rightly so. Dave's books are written to the middle class; this book is for people who are determined not to remain there. More than a book about money, this is a book about life. And while it does have a strong 'religious right' flavor, it is packed with practical advice and compelling information."

- Todd Sivers, IncredibleAdvantage.com

ABOUT THE AUTHOR

Larry Jones is the Generosity Pastor of First Baptist Raytown, Missouri, located in the Kansas City Metro Area. Larry first joined the staff in 1999 as the Associate Minister of Music. After life-changing experiences with Crown Financial Ministries (2000) and Dave Ramsey's original Financial Peace book (2004), he found himself with an extra staff role in the area of stewardship in 2008. This second role came about as a result of living out the principles that are taught by Crown Financial and Financial Peace — creating financial margin with cash reserves, debt free living, wise investing, and generous giving.

As a writer, Larry has been a successful serial blogger for almost a decade. He has also written a couple of smaller eBooks. *Heroic Personal Finances for Christians* is his first long-form personal finance, self-help book. *Heroic Personal Finances: 3 Steps To Become A Money Hero* is his second book in the series.

Larry's mission is to help as many people as possible move into a state of abundance and generosity in their lives. Life is too short, and there's too much to accomplish. People need to shed the shackles of debt and poor financial thinking and move to a place of prosperity so that they can help more people.

When Larry isn't writing or performing his Generosity Pastor duties, he is directing a 37-member volunteer worship orchestra at First Baptist Raytown.

Larry currently lives in Lee's Summit, Missouri, with his amazing wife Jennifer, four beautiful daughters, and one handsome son.

Here's how you can connect with Larry:

- LinkedIn: https://www.linkedin.com/in/joneswlarry
- Facebook: https://www.facebook.com/larryjones.biz
- Twitter: @JonesWLarry
- Google+: https://plus.google.com/u/0/104214976165798488810/posts
- Book Website: HeroicPersonalFinances.com

ENDNOTES

Introduction

[i] Source: http://www.dictionary.com/browse/hero

Step #1: Capture the Vision, Then Make a Decision

[ii] Source:
https://www.biblegateway.com/passage/?search=Proverbs+29%3A18&version=KJV

[iii] Source: http://www.goodreads.com/quotes/57938-everything-begins-with-a-decision-then-we-have-to-manage

---

Chapter 1: The Vision Thing

[iv] Source: http://www.thisdayinquotes.com/2011/01/george-hw-bush-and-vision-thing.html

---

Chapter 2: Burn the Ships!

[v] Source: http://www.goodreads.com/quotes/57938-everything-begins-with-a-decision-then-we-have-to-manage

[vi] Source: https://www.ideaconnection.com/blog/2014/04/open-innovation-commitment/

Step #2: Create a Plan, Then Take Action

[vii] Source:
https://www.brainyquote.com/quotes/quotes/a/andrewjack163004.html

[viii] Source: http://www.singlefounder.com/losers-have-goals-winners-have-systems/

[ix] Source: https://www.brainyquote.com/quotes/quotes/t/tonyrobbin147791.html?src=t_goals

Chapter 8: Systems Are the Key

[x] Source: http://www.singlefounder.com/losers-have-goals-winners-have-systems/

Step #3: Concentrate On the Front End, But Control Your Backend

[xi] Source: https://www.brainyquote.com/quotes/authors/s/sophia_amoruso.html

[xii] Source: https://www.entrepreneur.com/article/248759

www.ingramcontent.com/pod-product-compliance
Lightning Source LLC
Chambersburg PA
CBHW061202180526
45170CB00002B/921